To Jean

November 15, 2016

Thank u for your support,
God bless u!

Marquis A. gorner

HAVE YOU EVER WISHED YOU WERE SOMEONE ELSE?:
Carrying the Weight of Autism

Marquis Garner

Orange Hat Publishing
www.orangehatpublishing.com - Waukesha, WI

DEDICATION

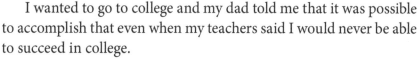

This book is dedicated to my dad, Steven A. Garner. I dedicate this book, to my father because as a young man, I feel blessed to have a father who is greatly involved in my life and believes in my dreams and aspirations.

When I have a goal or dream that I set my mind to, my dad does not say that my dream is impossible to accomplish. He believes in me and helps me to achieve it.

I wanted to go to college and my dad told me that it was possible to accomplish that even when my teachers said I would never be able to succeed in college.

When I told my father I wanted to try out for pro basketball my father helped me make that dream possible. My dad helped me start an internet campaign www.gofundme.com to make the publication of this book possible.

I feel blessed to have my father in my life. He has been there for me in the important moments in my life.

The best moment I had with my father is when we graduated together from Bible College in 2007. We walked across the stage together and received our degrees in biblical studies.

That, is a moment no one can ever take away from me. and I am grateful to him more than words can say for helping make it happen.

Thanks for all the memories Dad, and for being the great man and person that you are. I dedicate this book to you.

I love you Dad,
Marquis A. Garner

ACKNOWLEDGEMENT

Writing my autobiography on autism, which I've been afflicted by since my birth, offered me the invaluable experience to undertake a challenge which broadened my communication skills, and allowed me to develop a business relationship, which continually grew as my book developed into a labor of love and a complex undertaking.

Sharing my story in print has been an exhilarating opportunity to be more open-minded and to accept the fact that each human being has a God-given talent, which if nurtured properly, will prosper to the extent that someone will take notice.

Someone did take notice of my idea of sharing my story and worked with me closely, offering suggestions, editing and proofreading. In that regard, I want to thank Nathan Conyers and the staff of The Milwaukee Times Printing and Publishing Company for their attention to detail and invaluable assistance.

I also want to thank Nathan Conyers for allowing me to share some of my essays in *The Milwaukee Times Weekly Newspaper*. He has been a true blessing from God. I thank him for his kindness and gratitude. I wish him and the staff of the Milwaukee Times Weekly Newspaper Printing and Publishing Company God's continued blessings.

CONTENTS

INTRODUCTION

Autism spectrum disorder (ASD) and autism are both general terms for a group of complex disorders of brain development. These disorders are characterized, in varying degrees, by difficulties in social interaction, verbal and nonverbal communication, and repetitive behaviors. With the May 2013 publication of the DSM-5 diagnostic manual, all autism disorders were merged into one umbrella diagnosis of ASD. Previously, they were recognized as distinct subtypes, including autistic disorder, childhood disintegra-tive disorder, pervasive developmental—not otherwise specified (PDD-NOS)—and Asperger syndrome.

ASD can be associated with intellectual disability; difficulties in motor coordination and attention; and physical health issues such as sleep and gastrointestinal disturbances. Some persons with ASD excel in visual skills, music, math and art. Autism appears to have its roots in very early brain development; however, the most obvious signs and symptoms of autism tend to emerge between two and three years of age. Autism Speaks continues to fund research on effective methods for earlier diagnosis, as early intervention with proven behavioral therapies can improve outcomes. Increasing autism awareness is a key aspect of this work and one in which our families and volunteers play an invaluable role.

Autism statistics from the United States Centers for Disease Control and Prevention (CDC) identify around 1 in 68 Americans on the autism spectrum—a ten-fold increase in prevalence in 40 years. Careful research shows that this increase is only partly explained by improved diagnosis and awareness. Studies also show that autism is more commonly diagnosed in males than females.

ASD affects more than 3 million individuals in the U.S. and tens of millions worldwide. Moreover, government autism statistics suggest that prevalence rates have increased 10 to 17 percent annually in recent years. There is no established explanation for this continuing increase, although improved diagnosis and environmental influences are two reasons often considered.

Not long ago, the answer to this question would have been, "We have no idea." Research is now delivering the answers. First and foremost, there is no one cause of autism just as there is no one type of autism. Over the last 5 years, scientists have identified a number of rare gene changes, or mutations, associated with autism. A small number of these are sufficient to cause autism by themselves. Most cases of autism, however, appear to be caused by a combination of autism risk genes and environmental factors influencing early brain development. In the presence of a genetic predisposition to autism, a number of non-genetic, or environmental, stresses appear to increase a child's risk. The clearest evidence of these autism risk factors involves events before and during birth. They include advanced parental age at time of conception (both mom and dad); maternal illness during pregnancy; and certain difficulties during birth, particularly those involving periods of oxygen deprivation to the baby's brain. It is important to keep in mind that these factors, by themselves, do not cause autism. Rather, in combination with genetic risk factors, they appear to increase risk modestly.

A growing body of research suggests that a woman can reduce her risk of having a child with autism by taking prenatal vitamins containing folic acid and/or eating a diet rich in folic acid (at least 600 mcg a day) during the months before and after conception. Increasingly, researchers are looking at the role of the immune system in autism. Autism Speaks is working to increase awareness and investigation of these and other issues, where further research has the potential to improve the lives of those who struggle with autism.

People always say, I don't look slow, or look like I have autism! That is because they don't understand that there are different levels and complexities of autism. What does it mean to be on the spectrum? Each individual with autism is unique. Many of those on the autism spectrum have exceptional abilities in visual skills, music and academics. About 40 percent have average to above-average intellectual abilities. Indeed, many persons on the spectrum take deserved pride in their distinctive abilities and atypical ways of viewing the world. Others have a significant disability and are unable to live independently. About 25 percent of individuals with ASD are non-verbal but can learn to communicate using other means. Autism Speaks' mission is to improve the lives of all those on the autism spectrum. For some, this means the development and delivery of more effective treatments that can address significant challenges in communication and physical health. For others, it means increasing acceptance, respect and support.

Marquis' parents on vacation in Florida.

Chapter I
A Mother's Story
by Tawanda Garner Payne

My son Marquis Antwan Garner came into the world two months early and weighing just two pounds. It was January 8, 1980 and was he unable to breath on his own. He required an incubator to assist his breathing.

I was thankful to God that Marquis was born in the 1980s, because the hi-tech incubator kept my son alive. I shudder to think that if he had been born just a few years earlier, he probably would not have lived.

Marquis was a sweet child growing up. He was always thinking of others before he thought of himself. By the time he was three-years-old, I knew that he was different than most children his age. I don't even remember Marquis having the 'terrible twos'. He was such a sweet, modest child.

When we would eat meals at the dinner table, Marquis would eat half of his meal and then stop. When I would ask him why he had not finished and remind him that he had to eat everything on his plate, if he wanted to grow up, to be tall and strong. Marquis at the age of three said the most profound, sweetest thing that, would warm any mother's heart, and make her proud. He would say: "Mom I don't care about being big physically, what is more important is the type of person I grow up to be. I want to grow up, to be a good person who treats people with respect. That is more important than being tall and strong. I was in awe, that my three-year-old son said that.

At that point I knew he was different but, I never suspected he had autism; I didn't know what autism was back then. There were other clues that my son was different. While other kids were obsessed with watching cartoons, my son was obsessed with watching basketball by the time he was four-years-old, he was listening to the singer Prince or Michael Jackson on the radio, all day.

As my son got older, relatives and friends always said that I was and still am too overprotective, but I always, tell them, it is my job to keep him safe and protected. I always tell Marquis "You are my son and when I'm dead and gone, I don't want anyone taking advantage of you."

Having a son with a disability, I think it is vital that, parents have the important discussion of what type of financial stability and life structure, their disabled child will have in the event that parents and/or other family and caregivers pass before the disabled person. I always tell Marquis to live his life, not to let his disability, stop him from living life to the fullest. Marquis, his dad and I have taken many vacations together, attended church retreats, and visited Disneyworld. Once we even appeared on a reality-court-room TV show together.

Giving birth to my son has been a wonderful experience for me. He loves to read the Holy Bible, to me, and he tells me that, he loves me a thousand times practically every day. These are things I love about Marquis and they are all positive things. And I will continue to focus on the positive and fun times I have with Marquis.

Because I feel that my son is a precious gift from God, I worry that wicked people might seek to take advantage of his innocence. If there have been times when I seemed too overprotective of Marquis, it is out of concern for his well-being among people he does not already know.

I am not sure that Marquis fully understands that not every person can be trusted. I have frequently talked to my son about how this is a cruel world we live in. And some people will mistake your kindness for weakness and try to take advantage of you.

Marquis is probably sick of hearing me say it, but I often tell him that you can't change people. Each person has their own heart and mind. You can tell people about God and invite them to church, but only God knows when and if they will ever be ready to submit and change their ways. I tell Marquis you can't save everyone. But you can change, the world, if you touch the life of at least one person. I am so proud of my son. I tell him, "Son, even if you only touch one life, by trying to make, a positive change in the world, than you have done your job."

I'm so proud of my son, and I want to protect him from the weight of this world which is designed to deny him his true potential. Being a young African American male, I tell him not to worry about the stereotypes some people may have of him. Because his father and I, his friends and the extended family know that he is a good person.

Marquis my pride, my joy, my son, has never had a bad record, never been to jail and I tell him that as an American citizen that is exactly, how I expect him to be: a well-to-do, law-abiding citizen.

I also try to reassure him not to worry about how his classmates treated him in school. Those experiences are part of his testimony.

So to sum all this up, I'm saying, that, the biggest blessing, in my life, occurred on January 8, 1980 that, is the day, that, I gave birth to my son born with autism. His name is Marquis A. Garner, and I love him with all my heart.

Chapter II
A Grandmother Introduces Marquis to the Bible
by Nancy Gordon

My name is Nancy Gordon. Marquis Garner is my grandson. His father, Steve, is my son. I remember the day that my son and daughter-in-law gave birth to my first grandchild. Marquis was a beautiful little baby with curly hair and little corrective glasses because he was cross-eyed. My little grandchild looked like a little professor with his glasses on.

When my grandson was one-year-old, I wanted, to instill in him, upright morals and principles. I taught him about the good book, also known as the Holy Bible. When my grandson, was learning how to read, I wanted to make sure that, the first book he knew how to read was God's word. When my grandson was four-years-old, his mother wanted to finish college, and his dad was in college and working. My grandson was with me 100 percent of the time.

My husband who was alive at that time would take us to the store or perhaps to a friend's house and I was so proud of my grandson, Marquis. He was such a well-mannered young man. I knew that reading the bible to him and taking, him to church helped teach him right from wrong as a toddler. Those lessons he learned at a young age helped make him into the respectable young man he is today. As a child I tried to teach him to be truthful and a good Christian. By the time Marquis, was born all my children were grown. I had raised all five children to adulthood. So when Marquis came into the world in the 1980s, I was happy, that, one of my five children had given me a grandchild, a beautiful caramel-skinned curly-haired boy.

He was such a beautiful baby that people would come up and say how beautiful he was. I would say: "Thank you, but I want to make sure my grandchild is, beautiful on the inside and knows Jesus. It will save him a world of trouble, if I put the love of Jesus in his heart. I want to save my grandchild from prison and the street life."

And by the grace of God, my grandson has never had a criminal record or been in, prison; thank you Jesus. My grandson was very quiet, quieter than most children his age growing up. When he was a child and even to this day, I tell Marquis that I don't believe in doctors or physiologists giving another human being, a label, for example telling another person that, they are slow, or different.

I always tell Marquis you are a human being, just like any other who has walked the face of this earth. You have two arms and two legs like anyone else. I tell him not to let anyone make you feel any less a person than they are I believe we are all equal in the eyes of God. No one is better than anyone else. When my grandson tells me that kids made fun of him in school and called him names like 'retard', I would just tell him you are a king. You were created in the image, of God, I know that, it, sounds like a cliché, but I don't believe in giving praises to a celebrity, or a famous person. I believe that, we are all equal in God's eyes I don't believe in rich, poor or middle class. Those are man-made ways of dismissing people who are different in some way and I don't live by that code.

I am a woman of God and I tell my grandson that he is a child of God. Yes, he may have autism, but I never let that diagnosis hinder him as a child and I have not changed my ways toward him. I tell him to use the autism that he was born with as a blessing and to live his life according to the rules statues and laws of God.

Once I asked my grandson what he considered to be the most important thing, in life. He said his goal was to educate people about autism, but even more urgently, he wanted to encourage others to live according to God's plan for us.

Another time I asked Marquis what his favorite bible verse was. He said Galatians 2:20 "I am crucified with Christ. It is not I that live, but Christ, who lives in me and the life, that, I now live in this flesh, I live by faith, in the son of God who loved me, and gave Himself up for me." As a grandmother, I couldn't be any prouder of my grandson. I must say that, he is a pure joy, to have, in my life.

CHAPTER III
No Rest for My Mind
by Marquis Garner

Have you ever wished you were someone else? I have wished I was someone else all the time. In the Old Testament book of Job, a man in despair named Job asks God a similar question. "Why was I born? Why didn't God make me stillborn in my mother's womb?"

Allow me to introduce myself. My name is Marquis Garner and I have a cognitive disability known as autism.

Throughout my young life, I have often asked God why He created me. Growing up with autism was certainly not easy, because at first glance, I don't fit the mold of a person with a disability. People who suffer from autism look pretty much like everyone else. I looked like your average 16-year-old African American male, but in fact I was born on January 8, 1980.

It took me 34 years to find out what my calling was; or perhaps I should say I knew what my calling was, but I put off telling my story until now. In high school I was described as being mentally ill.

The other students made fun of me because I looked like them and therefore they could not understand why I was in the Special Education program.

My mind could not find a place to rest. It was as if I could feel the weight of my disability squeezing the breath out of my lungs.

It is a very strange feeling when people who don't even know you try to put a label on you. They have no idea what kind of hardships might be the cause for the stranger. We are all human beings and l hope all people come to know Jesus before they die.

I have been to numerous funerals. Sometimes I wonder what the purpose of life is – if once you are gone, you and your work are soon forgotten.

It's easy to get caught up pursuing individual ambitions, but in the end, the context of eternity is all human arrogance. Boasting what we are going to accomplish or about the possessions we own means we truly don't understand life. Until we understand that we have nothing of any value.

More than half of school-aged children are age five or older when they are first diagnosed with autism spectrum disorder, according to the results of a study published in 2012 by the National Center for Health Statistics Data Brief.

Educators and medical professionals are capable of reliably diagnosing autism in children as young as two, according to chief science officer at Autism Speaks Geraldine Dawson, PhD, who was interviewed by WebMD. Dr. Dawson believes that autistic children who receive early educational intervention and speech therapy tend to do better in the long run.

I remember like it was yesterday when I was told that I had autism and that I would have to be placed in a special education class.

Actually I remember two different occasions when I was told I was different from the 'norm'. I started Kindergarten in the Milwaukee Public School System, attending MPS schools through the third grade.

I was held back in the first grade, because my teachers thought I was not trying hard enough to master the curriculum. My teachers did not realize that I needed extra special assistance.

I went to a Catholic elementary school in the fourth grade. I soon discovered that the lessons and the pace of learning at my new school was 10 times more advanced than what I was used to at my old school. I could not learn the curriculum at the same pace as my peers so my teachers had a meeting with my parents.

*Marquis in kindergarten in a Christmas pageant
at Atonement Lutheran School.*

Marquis celebrating his eighth birthday party at Chuck E. Cheese.

My teacher thought my slow learning ability was due to a lack of motivation or focus. The teacher told my parents, my slow learning process could have been made worse by a poor early education.

In order to help me catch up my teacher and parents came to the conclusion that while all my friends were outside playing fun games I had to stay inside and get privately tutored by the school principal.

While my friends, were having the time of their lives playing outside. I cried in front of my principal. I told him, I was missing the best times of my life. I had to stay inside and get tutored, by him, because God didn't make me smart enough.

"I don't know why He created me. He must not like me," I said. My principal told me not to worry. "Marquis God loves you and to be honest with you, you have changed my life and you are making a difference in a positive way, just by me tutoring and helping you."

I thanked the principal and shook his hand. His encouraging words have stayed with me ever since. I finished fourth grade, but when a stranger tried to break into our apartment, while my mom and I were at home and my dad was at work, we had to move as a matter of personal safety.

After we moved I wasn't able to go back to my Catholic school. I began fifth grade in my new middle school but I kept falling further and further behind in my studies. My teacher had a meeting with my parents and told them that on a test about the geography of the United States I had only been able to identify two out of the 50 states correctly.

The teacher told my parents that I had a long time to study, two weeks. My parents, told the teacher that I had studied. The teacher suggested I get tested, to see if I had a learning disability.

My teacher and parents scheduled an examination, to determine my educational level, as well as my mental, physical, and emotional health. The test, called an "M team test" indicated that my IQ was borderline mentally retarded now called intellectually disabled out of respect for people.

I would get nervous around a classroom full of kids and feel the need to vomit. My behavior seemed odd to other children, and I met with a therapist who tested me in the sixth grade. That was when I was finally correctly diagnosed as cognitively disabled

Sixth grade photo at Bayside Middle School.

with autism. Sometimes I would just sit in my room, and tell my mom that I wanted to be by myself. My mom asked me, if I was upset about my disability. I told her that I was not. "I'm just upset that, these so called experts could be so wrong about why I was having trouble learning my school work."

Chapter IV
A Face in the Crowd
by Marquis Garner

When I was a child in school, I didn't understand the meaning of life. Most young people live entirely in the present. Most children are oblivious to their future. They may daydream about what they want to be when they grow up, but very few make a plan and follow it through to success.

Like most kids, I only lived in the here and now, and all I could see was that I was in a special education class and bullied. I thought that was going to be my reality for life. When kids form a negative opinion about you, it's hard for you to get them to change their mind.

The reason I know that to be true, is because in fifth grade, one of the young people in my math class looked at me, and whispered, "The gym teacher said 'the reason why Marquis can't play sports as good as us, is because he was born premature and his brain doesn't understand things the way we understand them, his brain don't connect the dots together to understand simple everyday things." My fellow students were whispering and chatting about me as if I couldn't hear them.

I cannot remember a time when having autism did not cause relationship problems with my classmates. In the second grade, the kids would scrutinize me, because I was too quiet, I wasn't vocal enough. The sad part about my situation is that I was not diagnosed cognitively disabled with autism until the sixth grade.

I attended a public elementary school that had too many students in the classroom. With so many students, I was just another face in the crowd. I couldn't get the individual attention that I needed. Some of the feelings I felt on the inside, as a kid, I couldn't understand; I would feel nervous and ill around other children. Often I became physically uncomfortable and would have to run to the bathroom. It got worse when I tried out for sports in high school.

When I tried out for the basketball team, I wound up in last place in the running drills. I had difficulty remembering plays. I had to try out for point guard, being five feet five inches and 135 pounds.

Once I remember scoring a basket on a nice spin move. I remember someone on the other team saying: "Come on man; he's in a retarded class. Don't let him score on you like that." This comment was on the first day of tryouts and I couldn't stop thinking about it.

I was so nervous and worried about making the team that I vomited everywhere in the bathroom stall after lunch at school the next day. This was the first time that I was ever that physically sick from worrying about not fitting in. I was cut from the basketball team.

The next year I tried out for the football team. It was a 'no cut' sport, but I felt as if I was the laughing stock of the junior varsity football team. I got into a game and to my surprise, I heard the coach on the other team telling his players not to touch me; that I was a special kid. "Don't cover him. He's in a disability class," I heard him screaming.

I couldn't believe what I was hearing. My eyes just scanned the scenery, taking in what people thought of me, when they looked at me. It was not a good feeling, but it was about to get much worse.

I was playing wide receiver and I was wide open in the end zone. No one was covering me. My quarterback looked through me like I was invisible. He did not pass me the ball and we didn't score.

That missed opportunity gave the other team good field position and they wound up scoring. After the game, I gave the quarterback a piece of my mind, "Come on man," I said. "Anyone can catch, why didn't you pass me the ball?"

"I didn't see you," he said.

Every year I tried out for the basketball team and every year I was cut. Soon after learning I'd been cut in my senior year I was depressed in the hallway commons, waiting for my mom to pick me up after school. One of my classmates from senior composition, named Deanna Thompson, a beautiful, young articulate African American female was chatting with some of her friends. She looked over and saw me looking sad. "What's wrong Marquis; why are you looking so sad?" she asked.

"Because I was cut from the basketball team," I said. She looked at me, and said, "Marquis, there is always next year."

"I'm a senior like you, there is no next year." I said.

"I'm sorry," she said. "You look so young I forgot you are in my class. Marquis don't worry about it. God will provide you with

Deanna Thompson

another opportunity."

"But Deanna," I said, "The other players on the team laughed at me and called me retarded."

"Don't worry about it, Marquis, God has you covered," she said. Then she gave me a smile so sincere and genuine, I tried to keep her spirit with me the rest of the year.

Chapter V
A Special Education
by Marquis Garner

I began suffering from a lot of anxiety. I hated to be around my classmates. The thought of them knowing I was in a special education class with autism and that I was a failure who was cut from the basketball team four years in a row, caused me to have negative thoughts and I would vomit a lot, and spent a lot of time in the bathroom. I was thinking about suicide, because I couldn't understand why God didn't let me die when I was a baby. I felt worthless.

My parents made me get professional help; I would see a psychologist every week, until I graduated. I have to say one of my teachers helped me get through the pitfalls of feeling like a failure in high school. But I think overall my special education teachers did a horrible job, as far as making sure I had a support system there for me.

There should be a high school support group for people with autism and other disabilities, a place where we can go to express our feelings. And there should be resources available for counseling and training, because a lot of children with autism get bullied, and tormented.

I have a disability, but I look normal so if I do something that seems odd to people, they may judge me, and even criticize me, because they think I'm acting that way on purpose. I hope by sharing my experiences of autism that parents can read this book with their children, and discuss with them their feelings about what it must be like to be constantly teased and bullied.

I had a major test that I thought would break me, during my sophomore year in high school. I was riding the regular bus with classmates who were not part of the special education program, and because of the stress and anxiety of being in class, one day I was late getting to the bus after school. I ran on the bus and I told the driver that I was sorry.

She looked at me and said: "We've been waiting for 10 minutes." I apologized again. That is when a girl on the bus embarrassed me in front of everyone.

"Marquis was late because he came all the way from the B-wing of the school for the slow people," she said.

I looked at her and told her to be quiet and mind her own business. I sat down, but inside I was hurting. I felt like I was walking around at school with a thousand pound weight on my shoulders, being in a special education class, I was not popular and all I wanted to do was to fit in.

The bus driver evidently did not forgive or forget my tardiness. One day she dropped me off very late, and my mother was worried because it was almost 6 pm and my mother knew I hadn't stayed after for any extracurricular school activities. I was one of the last people on the bus. There were only three others left. I don't know what the bus driver was thinking, but she kept dropping person after person off before me, and I kept saying, "Excuse me, you keep passing my stop."

She kept saying she was going to drop this person off before me today. "I'll get you home, don't worry!" she said.

I was quiet for the rest of the ride. When she finally pulled over at my stop it was about three hours past the time I was supposed to be home. I got up to get off the bus. She looked at the girls on the bus and said, "Marquis is still on the bus, he was so quiet, I forgot he was still here. He's been so quiet. I was going skip his stop and keep going."

I was upset when she said that, because I had told her I needed to be home, or my mom would be worried. I walked to the front of the bus, upset. "What do you mean you would have skipped my stop? I told you I needed to be home first or my mother would be worried."

The bus driver made some hurtful remark as if my feelings didn't matter. I believe she called me slow and made fun of my autism, because I heard a girl on the bus laugh.

"What did the bus driver say to Marquis?" one girl asked.

"Told him to get his slow butt off the bus and go home," another girl said laughing.

I was about to walk off the bus, when I turned around and looked at the bus driver. "Did you call me slow?" I asked her.

She just laughed. "Boy get your butt off the bus. Don't worry about it."

I looked at her and said, "You were going skip my stop when I told you, I needed to be home. Then you drop me off late and disrespect me by calling me slow."

She said something and laughed. I walked up to her face and

said shut up nappy head, and touched her hair. I knew I should not have touched her, but I didn't hit her. She gave me an evil look, like I'm going to get him.

The next day, my bus didn't show up before my mother left for work, and it was just my father and me at home. He had prepared breakfast and he started wondering why my bus hadn't shown up.

"Why didn't your bus come to pick you up? You must have done something," he said.

"I didn't do anything," I replied.

About an hour later we received a call from the high school principal. "Mr. Garner you need to come up to the school quick," the principal said. "I need to have a meeting with you and Marquis. He did something very bad and I'm thinking about expelling him from school for good. If I do he won't be allowed back."

"What did he do?" my father asked. "Can you tell me over the phone?"

The principal said it was very bad and that he would rather discuss it in person.

My dad began demanding to know what I had done that would make the principal want to meet with us in person.

"Tell me what you did, now," he said to me. "I don't want to go up here to this high school and be embarrassed." I told him that the bus driver called me slow and embarrassed me in front of the students, and that she skipped my stop.

I also told him that I had touched the bus driver's hair. My dad gave me a good old-fashioned whipping, which left marks on my back. When we got to the high school, the bus driver was also in the principal's office, but her story was not accurate. She said I got up to get off the bus and back-handed her in the face for no reason, and that she was going to see a doctor because she thought I might have broken a bone in her face.

I was furious when the principal gave me a chance to tell my side of the story. I said: "She's lying. I didn't slap her. I told her that I needed to be home, because my mother would be worried about where I was. She usually drops me off at home at 3:00 p.m. She didn't drop me off at my home until 6 p.m. When I got home my mother was worried sick.

"I have no cell phone, I said. "I had no way to communicate to my mother that I would be home that late. I told the bus driver and she ignored me and kept skipping my stop, and to add insult to injury, she made a sarcastic remark when she finally did get to my stop. She told the other people on the bus: "Marquis is still here? He's so quiet, I was going to skip his stop and keep going."

"After I had already sat on the bus for three hours I'm sorry Mr. Principal," I said, "but I feel like she totally disrespected me. Then as I was exiting the bus, I didn't say anything to her, I didn't disrespect her, but she disrespected me. I heard one of the girls laughing and asking the bus driver what she had just said.

"Did you tell Marquis to get his slow retarded butt off the bus?" the enraged principal asked the bus driver? "Did you say that? Did you call Marquis retarded? That is very inappropriate. Marquis is a young teenage kid and you are an adult.

"That is very inappropriate to have that type of interaction between you and a young teenager on your bus. You are an adult and Marquis is a student. I would hope you would know better than to have that type of inappropriate interaction with him."

The bus driver said she didn't call me retarded. "I called him slow," she replied.

"That is not appropriate for you to say," the principal remarked. "I could call the bus company you work for and report you. I am very disappointed that you would say that to one of our students who represents our high school. Marquis represents this high school just as much as any other student that is walking around this campus.

"You said Marquis slapped you in the face!" the principal continued. "Did he slap you in the face?" he asked.

"Well, he really didn't slap me," the bus driver confessed. "He touched the top of my head."

"Did he slap you, yes or no?" the principal persisted.

"No he didn't," she admitted.

My father looked at the principal and the bus driver and said: "Both of you owe me an apology". "I just disciplined my son beating him with a rod, for nothing. I thought he'd done something wrong. You both owe me an apology for having me come up to this high school for this meeting for nothing. I want an apology," he said, looking at the principal with a stern face. "I know my son has a disability, but he's not a bad kid."

"I'm sorry" the principal said looking at my father with a serious face. The principal then looked at the bus driver. "I think you owe Marquis and his father an apology, especially Mr. Garner, Marquis' father, for wasting his time. I'm sure he needs to be back at work."

The bus driver looked at me first. "I'm sorry Marquis," she confessed. Then she looked at my Dad and said: "I'm sorry sir. I'm sorry Mr. Garner for lying about your son and wasting your time."

We all shook hands and parted ways. I went to class, my father gave me a hug and apologized for beating me, and he treated me to dinner at Red Lobster that night in order to make amends.

I thank God that I believe in his son Jesus Christ. Some of the things that happened to me, I'm surprised I've lived to tell.

Marquis graduating from high school.

Definition of a Dream
Dedicated to the Rev. Dr. Martin Luther King, Jr.
By Marquis Garner

What is the definition of a dream?
You want me to tell you what the definition of a
dream means?

Martin Luther King had a dream.
We as black men need to step up, and take the
lead.

Treat our black women like queens.
Be the real men God said that, we are supposed to
be.
We should not disgrace our community.
We should show that, we know true unity.

Don't use derogatory language, calling our women
profane names.
Listen to our elders, because they most likely
boycotted and made it possible,
For us to sit anywhere on the bus.
So remember you can kill, the revolutionary, but
you can't kill the revolution.

Dr. King had one method: he wanted us to live in
peace, love and harmony.

And he said: If we know who God is and what God wants, Peace love and harmony shouldn't be a hard solution.
Now that, is the definition of Dr. King's dream for us to live together in paradise.

Dr. King may not be here anymore physically.
But if we live out his methods, he will always reign supreme.
Because he followed the personification of the true King.
This is the definition of Dr. King's dream.

Marquis enjoying extracurricular activities, such as playing a game of pool.

Marquis graduated from Midwest Bible College in 2007.

Marquis with his mom's mother and dad's mother at his graduation in 2007.

Marquis' Grandma Nancy and Marquis's Dad

Cousin Larry

Marquis with his Special Olympics team

Marquis with his Special Olympics team

Cousin Tammie with her son Miles

Aunt Tori and Grandmother Ruby

Marquis at his graduation from the Midwest Bible College

Dad and Marquis at their graduation

Marquis' family, The Dunlaps

Marquis' great grandmother at her 100th birthday with family

Marquis' family celebrated his great grandma's 100th birthday in South Carolina.

Marquis' parents with Packer's player Kabeer Gbaja-Biamila

Marquis' Mom and Cousin Jasmine

Family: Aunt Terri, Mom, and Aunt Tori

Family: Cousin Leica and Aunt Greta

Marquis and Cousin Alicia

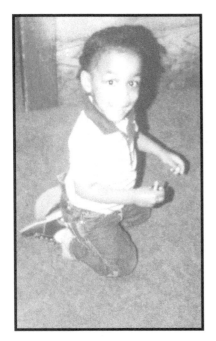

Marquis, age 3   *Cousins Joey and Miles*

*Grandmother and Cousin
Jasmine*

Mom and Aunt Pam with friend

Marquis visits family in South Carolina.

Marquis' Mom and Cousin Julie

Marquis' Mom with family on his dad's side

Chapter VI
Through the Storm
by Marquis Garner

Every year I would become very depressed when I was cut from the basketball team. I would try out, get cut, and be depressed for the rest of the year. Tryouts were only three days long, but my every consuming thought would be about what I had done wrong to not make the team. I was particularly upset with myself, because at the YMCA, I was a basketball sensation.

I played basketball every day at the southwest YMCA with my cousin Omarr. I was 17, playing against guys in their late 20s and early 30s, some of whom had played college ball, and I was the star. I would kill those guys, hitting 12 jump shots in a row, killing them with my nice spin move to the basket.

Every year when I would tell my cousin that I was cut from the basketball team, he would say, "I'm sorry you have some type of mental problem. When you play those guys at the YMCA you are the best player on the court. I can't understand why you can't make your high school basketball team. I think you have the talent. It's all in your head. You have to believe in yourself. Believe in your own abilities. It's all on you. You have to look yourself in the mirror and believe in yourself."

I tried everything my cousin told me, but I just couldn't get myself to perform well enough at high school tryouts. I thought maybe my failure was due to my autism, because I would practice basketball all year long, taking over the games right up until the tryouts. Then on the day of the tryouts, I would play like I was a beginner. I would miss jump shots and easy layups.

Once I was told by a gym teacher to use mental visualization to help perform better. I tried and it helped when I played at the YMCA, but in tryouts or a real game, I was terrible. I think part of the problem is my brain could never concentrate on one thing at a time. I put pressure on myself because I wanted to be a big basketball superstar, because I wanted to prove to the kids at school that I was more than just a guy with autism in a special education class.

I went to a psychologist because I couldn't take it anymore. I felt like I worked hard at academics and at sports, and I wasn't getting anywhere. I asked the psychologist why I played like a superstar at the YMCA, but not in real games. He said it could be part of my autism, and he performed with me mental visualization drills. He told me to have positive thoughts and repress my negative thoughts, or listen to my favorite piece of music or write when I had negative thoughts.

I tried everything he told me, but the negative thoughts still came. I found my mind dwelling on my failure. I asked God to let my late uncle Travis Payne visit me in my dreams, because I wanted to die. I didn't understand my purpose on earth. I felt like I was just taking up space. During my freshman year of high school, I felt like I was in a boring boarding school. I never participated in anything, just went to school, and came home. I didn't go to prom, or anything.

My uncle, Travis Payne, did come to me in a dream. He told me to be strong, and hang in there. In the dream, he asked me a very profound question. He asked: "If I thought I could make it through the storm?" I told him that I didn't know. My Uncle Travis had reminded me how I had made it through the storm, when our family received the sad news that he had been stabbed to death, while on his job in California. I had to remind him that I had to get professional help when he died, and that I have never really gotten over his death.

An important figure in Marquis' life is his uncle, Ronnie Dunlap, with whom he attended Parklawn Assembly of God Church each Sunday.

Uncle Travis reminded me that he would always be with me in spirit and that while his death was tragic, death is something that every human being on earth will face. We were born as an individual person, and we will die as an individual person. Then Uncle Travis said he didn't want me to concentrate on the circumstances of his death. He said he wanted me to "concentrate on being strong," like he was.

"The person who killed me, killed only my physical body. He didn't touch my spirit or soul," Uncle Travis said, adding, "Remember Marquis, your spirit and soul will live on forever even after your physical body is dead." Moreover, he explained that I had to be strong for Uncle Travis. That can only be done by me getting to know God and having a strong soul and spirit like his son, Jesus Christ, and "that way you will see me again Marquis," he explained.

"Right now, while your physical body is still walking on the earth, I need you to be strong for me and for your mother, who loves you with all her heart. I was the youngest in the family. I was her younger brother. I need you to be strong for everyone," he said to me in the dream.

"Marquis we will not understand everything we go through on earth, but remember God is sovereign." Those are the last words I remember my Uncle Travis saying to me in my dream, but after he was done talking we had his famous tuna fish sandwich which he was so excellent at making. We chatted and laughed, but I couldn't make out what we were saying while sitting at the kitchen table. When we finished eating lunch together, the dream ended.

I thought I would have an easier life after that visit from Uncle Travis. It felt so heavenly, but more problems would come. I was playing basketball at the YMCA. One day, and I was scoring on this guy, killing him, crossing him over, making him slip and slide, and his friends were making fun of him, so he started fouling and grabbing me by my shirt, becoming extra aggressive. We got into a shoving match. An older gentleman broke up the scuffle on the court and I apologized to the young man, and shook his hand.

But in the locker room he and four of his friends jumped me and beat me up. I must have suffered a concussion, because I forgot where I was, and ended up being taken to the hospital. A police officer came to my house and asked if I wanted to press charges. I said no and that God would take care of the situation.

Uncle Travis with his arm around Marquis at family reunion.

Chapter VII
Deliver Me, Lord
by Marquis Garner

I signed up for technical college. I wanted to take a computer class. When I was 15, I came up with an idea for a video game, and I thought I might be able to develop more.

I wanted to take learning the computer further. I scored low on the placement test, which said I was at a sixth grade level, so I had to go to the learning center every day, to do my homework, and to get my skills caught up, but I struggled to keep up with the basic concepts in my computer class. My mother paid a woman to be my tutor in the class but she could only help me so much, and I wasn't advancing in the class. Eventually I had to drop it.

I felt bad because I was 21 years old and had just dropped out of technical college with no job and seemingly no legitimate future for myself. I worked at the YMCA, but I didn't see that as a career. I liked the free membership, but I hated working for other people. I always felt as if people believed that they could speak to me disrespectfully.

We're all just human beings. The only good experience I remember from going to technical college is that I met a man who worked for Campus Crusade for Christ. His name was Mike Nabena.

He would become like a big brother to me. He took me on Christian retreats and we studied the Bible together. Once my parents got to know him, he would occasionally spend the night at my house, and I would spend the night at his house. He was the greatest. He was like the big brother I always wanted.

He even helped me achieve a dream on my 'bucket list'. We visited South Africa, my dream trip. Yes I was on the plane with Mike and my father all 26 hours of the flight to South Africa. I had the opportunity to visit Robben Island where Nelson Mandela was imprisoned for 27 years. I had the opportunity to pray for sick children affected by the HIV virus and full blown AIDS at an orphanage in Cape Town.

My father really broke down when he saw how children were living. One of the little girls I was hugging and telling her that I loved her and that God loves her more than me or anyone else, we learned of her being found behind a shopping mall in a garbage dump, crying.

Apparently she was only about four days old when she was found and been born HIV positive.

Now at age six she had full blown AIDS. That really broke my dad down, and it broke me down as well. I was upset too, because I hated that those children had to experience that type of life, being born innocent into a situation that they had no control over and didn't understand what was happening to them.

They were born with a disease that would kill them most likely before they reached adulthood. Most of them lived in little shanty houses with no running water.

After that trip I began to appreciate what I had and not to complain so much. That was 2008, and the year before that my dad believed in me so much that he flew me out to Long Beach, California to try out for the NBA basketball summer pro league. I had trained, lifted weights, and run on the treadmill every day, drowning in sweat.

I played terribly and was cut again, but I thank God for the experience. That is something I can keep with me for the rest of my life. I had the opportunity to try out for the NBA and I scored one point. Even though it was only the NBA Developmental League, I am still thankful for that experience.

I tried out with unknown players, free agents and restricted free agents. I didn't play against any mega-stars. I had the chance to try out for pro basketball and to go to Africa, so I'm thankful.

At this point you may be wondering, what does that have to do with autism? I think it has a lot to do with it. Through my failures and pain, I still have to try to live and enjoy my life.

I joined an organization called Flying for Faith. We had a private plane at Timmerman Field in Milwaukee. We could use activation to tell inner city kids about Jesus Christ.

Life was good in 2007. My parents had their own mortgage business in Brookfield and I was working with the Department of Vocational Rehabilitation, an organization that helps adults with disabilities find and retain jobs, but I didn't need help finding a job then because my parents had a successful mortgage company, and I worked for them.

They successfully ran their business from 2003 until 2008 when the housing industry collapsed along with the rest of the

Marquis works with his father, Steve Garner, and Mike Nabena at The Mortgage Group.

world economy and my parents had to sell their business.

We all make mistakes in life and I believe that there are times when it is important to own up to them. One of my regrets is that when I was younger I did not work with the Department of Vocational Administration. I told employers who hired me about my disability, before getting hired, but I should have worked with the DVR after I was hired, because I would have had a job coach, someone with whom I could talk things over and figure out the right way to respond to unfamiliar situations.

Dedication to Nelson Mandela
From Political Prisoner to President in Four Years
By Marquis Garner

Freedom fighter is what they call me, freedom fighter, is what I symbolized to the world.

God used me, or should I say, God worked through me in human form, to share the power
Of his forgiveness and love.

When you despair that, the sin you had committed was insurmountable,

Our great, God was still ready to forgive.

All you have to do is smile, and look at the example of my life.

And you will truly, understand that, God forgives.

Although my physical life has ended don't mourn for me, but rejoice.

Rejoice in the fact that, I defied fate:
I went to prison in my 40s,
Served 27 years and was released after I had turned 70 years-old.

And still the Lord used me to accomplish a miracle.
I went from political prisoner to President of South Africa in four years.

The lord blessed me with 95 years of life on this Earth.

New generations touched by the spiritual journey God led me to do.
But now the savior has called me home.
Remember if you live for peace, love, forgiveness, and acceptance, my legacy and memory will never vanish.
It will be eternal like the great Father I believe in.
He who is, was and always shall be.

Sincerely yours,
South African Political Prisoner
and former President
Nelson Rolihlaha Mandela aka Madina

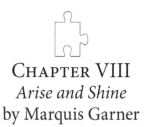

CHAPTER VIII
Arise and Shine
by Marquis Garner

I know that I'm not the only person with autism who has been depressed, suicidal, or felt like a complete failure. I hope I can connect with others who have the same feelings that I had and still have sometimes. It would be helpful to be able to connect with people who face difficulties similar to mine and to make some new friends. We can only become stronger when people with these issues and problems get help. The difficulties of adjusting to a life with autism need to be discussed and taken seriously. I want people to see beyond my illness. I try my best to live and enjoy life like anyone else.

Years after high school, I again ran into Deanna Thompson, that very beautiful young lady who comforted me after I had been cut from the basketball team in my senior year. I told her how much her comforting words had meant to me when I was down. She gave me a hug. I would see her several more times at the hospital where my father and I volunteered as chaplains and each time she would wave and say hello to my father and me. The last time I saw Deanna alive I walked past her as she was getting in an

Deanna Thompson

elevator. I heard someone yell, "Hi Marquis." I looked and it was her with that big beautiful wide smile. I returned the greeting, and she spoke to my dad as well. Then we went our separate ways.

That was on June 27, 2009. I happened to be on Facebook a little later on that day. Someone had written on their Facebook page that God had taken another beautiful soul to heaven, "Rest in peace Michael Jackson, Ed McMahon my Aunt Sue, and Deanna Thompson." When I read that, I went to her Facebook page, and I saw it was true. I felt like someone pulled my heart right out of my chest, because I kept visualizing her smiling at me with that big smile. I thought, "No God, not her. No."

Later I found out she was at the Milwaukee Summer Fest outdoor music concert where she had met her boyfriend to watch Frankie Beverly and Maze. She left the concert around midnight, said goodbye to her boyfriend, who was in a separate car. Somewhere along the way home, Deanna, who was only 29 years old at the time of her death, was hit and instantly killed by an intoxicated 29-year-old man.

I went to the repast with my father at St Mark AME Church in Milwaukee, because of the impact of the crash she did not look like the young woman I remembered. I didn't stay for the funeral. I was very upset. I didn't understand at the time why God would allow something so dreadful to happen.

About five years after her death, I met Deanna's father. His name is Ronny Thompson, and he had started Athletes for Autism in memory of Deanna. He has a gym where he works with autistic youth and adults. Many high school kids with autism and other disabilities aren't always accepted, so a lot of times we just sit

Meeting Ronny Thompson must have been by divine intervention. I attended school with his daughter who was killed in a car accident. Ronny founded a program, Athletes for Autism, after the passing of his daughter, Deanna.

around the house with no job, and not being productive at all.

I believe I met Ronny because of a divine intervention, because of God. If it had not been for the death of Deanna, Ronny would never have begun his work with individuals like me who are affected by autism.

He had no reason to care about someone with autism, because he didn't know anyone affected by the disease, but after going to grief counseling and being depressed because of the untimely death of his daughter, he said God spoke to him one day, and told him to make a difference in the world by helping people affected by autism.

One day as we were riding in the car together, he said: "Marquis, death is not a bad thing. It can be looked at as a beautiful thing. When someone dies, they are transitioning to the next phase in life. My daughter's spirit is right here in this car, with you and me, and she is smiling at us. She is my angel."

I had a second visionary dream. My mother and I were running through a field. We had just fled from a bar. A man was running after us with a gun. I was eight years old. I felt bad, because we were running. I wanted to turn around and fight the man, but he had a gun. My mind was racing with a million thoughts, if I'm a little kid, why am I running? Shouldn't my mother be running for her life holding me in her arms? But it was too late to think further. I had to run for my life. In the dream I tripped over a rock and suddenly the man with the gun was standing over me.

"Don't shoot my son." my mother pleaded. Just then the man pulled the trigger and I heard the gun click. And the lights went out. I woke up in a cold sweat, alone in my bed. I realized it was a dream, and that I was not eight, but 16-years-old. I awoke in confusion, because I didn't understand the meaning of that dream. I prayed and asked God to give me a revelation of that dream.

After about six weeks, God showed me what that dream meant. Because of my autism I had always viewed myself as being weak and of no value, but God showed me that I do have worth and that it is my job to be a protector to my mother when my dad is not around. I may not think like my mom, but physically God revealed to me that I am physically stronger than her. My mother has a strong personality and she doesn't back down from anyone. I have to be on guard and protect her and let people know that I will protect her.

If I had to sum up my life, I would have to say it has been great. I think having autism is my testimony. God wants to use me as an example. No matter how many times people put me down, no matter how many times I fail; I just have to keep living my life and enjoy it while I can.

I remember all the pitfalls that happened in my life, but without the pitfalls and failures, I wouldn't have cherished the amazing events in my life, like my trip to Cape Town, South Africa with my father, or trying out for the NBA Developmental League, or being part of Voice of the Fatherless Child, a not-for-profit organization dedicated to preventing domestic violence in Milwaukee. This organization was started by Monte Mabra, a former inmate who changed his life around and started this organization to tell young black males about the importance of staying out of jail, being good fathers and taking an active interest in the lives of their children.

No deadbeat dads. Children need both parents and a stable family life to reach their full potential. Strong families will stop the cycle of young kids getting into trouble.

Having autism makes me aware of many overlooked problems in the world. It has also made me more compassionate about the suffering of others. I was treated so badly as a child because of my autism that it has made me sensitive to people who are considered outcasts in our society, the poor, the sick and others who suffer.

I knew a friend who was shot wrongfully by a police officer. I lost my Uncle Travis in a violent death. I lost my high school friend Deanna Thompson. Even though she was not around all the time, she spoke words of encouragement to me, every time we crossed paths, so she had a profound impact on my life.

Marquis Garner at Athletes for Autism event April 16, 2014 with Athletes for Autism founder, Ronny Thompson. Left to Right: Greg Garner, Ronny Thompson, Steve Garner (Marquis' dad) and Marquis Garner

The Essence of a Black Woman
By Marquis A. Garner

As a black woman sits staring at herself in the mirror,
I sit and stare and look in bewildered amazement,
Because the mirror doesn't define who you are as a black woman.

Your beauty runs more than skin deep,
Your inner beauty as a woman outweighs what society views as physical perfection.
Your aura and specimen define the greatness inside of such a woman

A woman who channels her indignation in order to press forward and raise a family often with little or no help from the father.

When she has no one to help, she presses forward and leans on God.

And that's why you are a beautiful black woman,
Because you have God on your side in your struggle to raise a boy to be a man.

Understand that if you believe in God,
You are never doing a difficult task alone.

You know how to fend for and nurture children, when a man is not around.

That is God-given.
You are a beautiful black woman.

Brothers should never call women a profane name.
Because most of us were raised, by single, reliable
women who went the distance to put food on the
table and roof over our head.
And that is the true essence of a real black woman.

So as you stand there and look at the reflection
of your face in the mirror. That others see when
they look at you. Understand beautiful, black
queen that beauty runs deeper than the physical
attributes that others see.

So rise sister, rise.
There are such beautiful magnitudes of dreams
that you display inside.
Flourish to reach that mountaintop
When others try to pull you down.

Just think of when you made it through more
difficult times. You are a beautiful woman. Just
look behind and see how many women desire to be
just like you: Strong, Committed, Dependable, and
Reliable

These words define the beautiful, true essence of
a remarkable woman and that woman is you.
Thank you black woman.

Marquis' Aunt Tori and his mom at the White Party during Summerfest in 2013.

CHAPTER IX
So Many Tears
by Marquis Garner

O nce during a question-and-answer session at an autism event sponsored by a university, someone in the audience asked me whether I dated girls. The answer is complicated. In 1995, my freshman year of high school, there was a beautiful young lady who showed an interest in me. We had ceramics class together and almost every day just the two of us would talk. We got to know each other better and I felt more and more confident being with her.

She told me that eventually we would go on a date. She told me where she lived and I longed for the day when we would go out on a date together. Like most teenagers I looked forward to having a relationship and doing things together with my girlfriend. Most of all I felt good when she was around or when I thought about her which, being a teenager, was very often.

My fine motor skills were still not fully developed and most of my ceramics projects were pretty terrible. One day the young lady that was my crush and who seemed to like me asked me why I had a paraprofessional helping me in the classroom. I explained to her that I had been born prematurely and that I was in a special education class.

It didn't seem to matter to her that I was in special education and so I opened up to her and told her about myself. We seemed to be getting along just fine right up to the day that she found out I got cut from the basketball team. After that things were never the same. She seemed to notice for the first time that there were students in my class with Down's syndrome and a variety of other learning disabilities. Pretty quickly she lost interest in me and started going out with a guy that was in the same grade. Everyone said he looked like me and it seemed as if everybody would get me confused with her new boyfriend. My heart was crushed every time people called me by his name.

One day as I was walking down one of the school hallways I looked up and saw the young lady from my ceramics class with the young man whom she was now dating. They were hugging, but I didn't see them at first, not until the young man called out to me: "Marquis, I heard you got cut from the basketball team. You should try out for Special Olympics," he said sarcastically. And then they both laughed. My ears burned with shame, but I was determined not to let them see how much they had hurt me.

I looked at them both directly in the eyes and said: "There is nothing wrong with a person participating in Special Olympics," as I kept briskly walking to my next class. I had not let them see my pain, but in my heart, I was hurting badly. I had tears, in my eyes as I walked away as fast as I could, and I was seriously depressed, the rest of the school year.

I would go and see a therapist, and chat, about my problems. I would tell, my therapist that, I never had a female friend. I feel like I got rejected at everything I attempt. I told her I wasn't good at anything and felt that, no girl, would want to be with, a young man in a special education class. My therapist would get me, to focus, on the, positive things in my life. The therapist would ask me, "Marquis what do you think, you are good at? I see that, you are a spiritual person, what do you think, the creator made you good at?"

So my therapist and I made a list of my abilities and skills. We both came to the conclusion that, I was a leader, in my special education class, and very, helpful, to the other students. When we finished my list, the therapist asked me "So Marquis, why are you afraid to ask someone out on a date when you meet a girl you like? I said that I just did not feel as though it was realistic for me to expect a girl to want to go out with someone in special education. I felt as if they would not be attracted to me, because of my disability.

My therapist than suggested I ask out a girl from my special education class. I told my therapist that I would keep that in mind. I was the only African American in my class, and I was concerned that maybe a young lady, in my class wouldn't feel comfortable with me asking them out. All the girls in my class were Caucasian, and I was nervous about that.

Eventually one of my friends in my class, asked me to go, to a clubhouse for youth aged 15-18. I met a young lady my age there, but she lived too far away. For a while I would chat, with her on the phone, but the relationship, never materialized.

I didn't go to my prom, or homecoming, in high school, so my older cousin got me to escort her best friend's niece to her prom, when I was 22 years old. It was at the Mitchell Park Horticultural

Conservatory dome, a beautiful building with exotic plants and a variety of flowers to ensure that there is almost always something in bloom. Many Milwaukee area high schools have proms, and high school reunions. Others use it for weddings and other special events.

I had, a good time, at that, prom until, the girl told me that she wanted to get married, have children and focus on family life. I told her that, I did not want to have children, and get married. After I said that she didn't speak to me. For the rest of the prom we sat in silence. It was only about two hours, but it felt like much longer. Again my confidence was shaken by how quickly a young woman lost interest in me over something I did or said.

I also felt bad that I had said I did not want to have children and I thought about that a lot. I eventually realized I had said that due to my fear of being rejected. With my lack of success starting a relationship with a young lady to being cut from the basketball team, I still felt like I was not, good, at, anything. And I didn't want my future wife, to regret marrying me because she thought I was unintelligent. Thinking about it now still brings tears to my eyes. I don't want my child, saying my dad is not smart enough to help me with my homework, so how can he help me, with my life problems?

I felt that, I couldn't win in any situation. I shared all of these thoughts and feelings with my therapist and he just told me, not to worry, about what people think of me. He said that, people are naturally negative, and that I should continue to focus on my positive qualities. My therapist told me, to focus on something like keeping, a journal, to help me not think, about the negative in my life.

I kept, a journal, that, helped, but the turning point came when I heard the song "So Many Tears" by the rap artist, Tupac Shakur. The lyrics describe the pain, in his life, but that song really helped me. When I listened to that song in high school it felt as if it had been written specifically about me and my pain.

When I listened to that song, my mind would think, about my Uncle Travis and the last time I talked with him before he died. Sometimes it would drift to other loved ones who had passed, and just life in general, my pain, and happiness, all of it seemingly contained in one little computer file of a four-minute long song.

I feel sad. Thinking about the overview, of my life, and I struggle staying positive, going to church and having my faith in, god, helps me. I just take life one day, at a time, and I am gradually growing more comfortable around, the opposite sex, one day, at a time. Life has always, been a hard test, for me, I always had my peers, telling me, I wasn't smart enough or good enough.

My peers saying that, I wasn't black enough, in terms of the way I acted. They think I don't act proud enough to be black and that I try to 'act white'. Other black males tell me I'm a 'chocolate boy'. They want to know why I'm trying to have curly hair when I'm not light skinned.

Because of my condition it seems as if every aspect of my life is always being inspected and judged negatively. I thank both of my grandmothers and my parents, for helping find my faith. It has helped me be at peace with myself.

If I get married, that, would be a beautiful thing, but right now, Jesus Christ is my foundation and my rock, I stand on solid ground because of him. Styles and fads, come and go. Sadly the same is true for people who come into your life and then leave.

My hope is in God, and his son Jesus. I have been praying for God to give me more confidence around women and hope his plan includes having a loving wife. Until then I will wait patiently until God says, I am ready for that to happen.

Marquis is pictured with Milwaukee Mayor Tom Barrett and
his friend of 20 years, James Patterson, at a special event.

The Nectar of My Fruit

The nectar of my fruit cannot be ruined, as long as I keep myself, motivated, or spiritually enticed.

The nectar of my fruit cannot be ruined, because I know that, my soul is too much into it.

Through my trials, and tribulations, I know that God has a plan for every human life.

Dear, God help me, live beyond the human ideologies, and all the strife.

I know that, putting my thoughts, on paper, has a purpose, through failure and pain, my strong spirituality, helped me get through the rain.

The nectar of my fruit awakens my soul, awakens the revolutionary, spirit in humanity, in me.

To make me realize that, we are all spiritually, connected, as one, one mind, one body, one heart.

If we don't realize, our connection, we have failed, our biggest test.
The nectar of the fruit was never meant to devise one plans or to divide or conquer.

We as the human race, only succeed when we know the definition of togetherness.
Once we understand that, method, we will be all right.

The nectar of my fruit, cannot, be ruined, or tamed. Because it was never meant, for us to think, we're better than someone else by putting down, another human being,.

The nectar, of my fruit cannot be ruined, because I want you all out there to know that my story, of growing, up, with autism, is not a mythology, it's a lived out true life story.

It's my story, Marquis A. Garner.
It's my reality.

Chapter X
Marquis, My Son
by Steven A. Garner

From the time my son was born my dream was that he would grow to be 6-feet-four-inches and weigh 210 pounds. I wanted my son to make it as a professional basketball player as soon as he came out of the womb. I work as a finance manager at a car dealership. I have been in sales for 35 years.

When my son was a toddler, I did not get to spend a lot of time with him because of my work schedule. When he was young I did not notice any signs of his disability. I just thought that he was a little behind on comprehension, but I did not think it was autism or any other kind of disability.

When we were married, Marquis' mother used to keep me informed about the daily activities of our son. As he got older, Marquis and his cousins started going to the YMCA so often that eventually they offered him a job.

I was very excited that things seemed to be falling into place for Marquis. Now that he was a teenager I was eager for him to try out for the basketball team. When I had time, I would help him with his game, going over the fundamentals. I thought for sure with all the practicing and playing that he was doing that he would make his high school team.

During his freshman tryouts Marquis' mother and I got married in Las Vegas. After the festivities with my wife and a few family members, I was looking forward to getting home, but before we left I called Marquis and asked him about the basketball tryouts.

Marquis seemed doubtful. He said he had missed a lot of jump shots in the tryout games. I told Marquis to think positively and reminded him that there were still a few days left of tryouts.

"Just think positive, focus, keep a clear mind and concentrate," I remember saying. Unfortunately when I returned home, I learned my son had not made the basketball team. I was devastated because I wanted the dream of my son becoming a professional basketball player.

You never want a child you brought into the world to feel rejected. I wanted my child's dream to become a reality. When I was not working, I helped my son prepare to try out for the basketball team in his sophomore year.

On car rides back and forth to the YMCA, I gave my son a lecture, on how important education is, and that I wanted him to be as smart as possible, because I wanted him to attend college. I was very proud of Marquis that year. Although he hadn't made the basketball team he did make dean's list both semesters. I was proud of my son's academic achievement. My wife and I treated our son to a beautiful five-star restaurant dinner for his academic achievement.

Although my son practiced basketball faithfully every day at the YMCA throughout his high school years, he wound up being cut all four years in a row from the team. Even more discouraging were the times when my wife and I would meet with my son's teachers.

By the time those depressing meetings were over, I was usually mentally drained. Part of the conferences involved discussing Marquis' Individualized Education Program (IEP), which is a written statement of the educational program designed to meet a student's individual needs.

Every student receiving special education services was required to have an IEP. My son's IEP reports were dreadful for me, to sit through. The teachers repeatedly said my son was performing at a 4th or 5th grade level, and the idea of him completing college was not realistic.

This was very painful for my heart to hear. Every year my wife and I would sit through those IEP meetings and hear the special education teachers lecture my wife and I about what my son was not capable of doing or achieving in life.

My wife was getting frustrated enough that sometimes she disagreed with the teachers.

After one meeting she was particularly upset because, Marquis' teachers had not said one positive thing about our son. So the next meeting when the teacher began their usual speech I interrupted.

"Well Marquis can't do this. He can't do that," one of them began. I said to the teacher: "You are telling me everything that my son cannot do, and you're being negative, do you have anything positive to chat with my wife and I about our son?

We want to hear something positive about Marquis," I scolded my son's teacher. "Is my son a nice guy? Is he a good kid? How well does he get along with his classmates? You spend eight hours a day, with my son, and you can't think of one positive quality that he has?"

The teacher's face turned red with embarrassment. "Oh Marquis is a very nice kid," the teacher said. "He is a sweet young man He's a leader in our special education class, but he struggles in the mainstream class. In order for Marquis to move on to higher education, it is vital for him to strive and do well in his mainstream classes."

My wife was very upset with our son's teacher. I told her not to worry about it, that I would handle the situation, I promised her our son would attend college and that we would set the bar high for Marquis and keep instilling in him that the Lord was on his side. That any dream in his heart was possible.

My son's teachers wanted him to be a 5th year senior because they felt that he was not ready for college. His academic level was too low to attend college.

At first I was ok, with the idea of my son being a 5th year senior, If it was going to improve his academic level, and get him the educational progress he needed in order for him to attend college I was all for it. My wife was very upset by the idea and after having a discussion with her about attending an extra year of high school, she refused to allow it.

So I had a chat with my son about going to technical college, to learn computers, I told Marquis that here was an opportunity to prove you can learn, just like everyone else.

Marquis struggled at the technical college and he eventually had to drop the computer programming classes in which I had prayed and asked God to help him succeed. I was very disappointed, but around this time Marquis, my wife and I had started attending to church faithfully.

Church helped me to maintain a positive attitude in the midst of my disappointment. One evening after church I said to my son, what do you want to do with your life? Since the computer programming didn't work out for you.

Marquis' answer touched my heart. The negative memory of all those depressing teacher meetings vanished like a puff of smoke.

It was clear from his response that Marquis had been thinking about this very same question for a while. He began:

"Well dad we attend church every week, and I'm really getting into the word of God and His Holy Bible. God said If we believe in his Son Jesus Christ and that he died on the cross for us, we shall be saved, and have eternal life. Dad, that is the most important thing in the world, knowing Jesus Christ so we can go to heaven and be together forever.

"And you know what, Dad? When we get to heaven I won't have a disability anymore. I will be perfect, like Jesus and my autism will be a thing of the past. Dad since you and I know that all things in this world are temporary and will pass away. We should go to Bible college together and get to know the word of God better together as father and son."

I agreed with my son wholeheartedly. The first year in 2006, I was not able to attend bible college with my son because I was helping my wife, his mother run the family mortgage business, but after going to a great Christian church conference with my family and being enlightened by the word of God, I attended bible college with my son in 2007 and we both earned our biblical studies degrees.

To see our son, who was repeatedly told that he would never be capable of attending college getting his bachelor's degree in biblical studies from a bible college, made me see that, with God all things are possible.

When I attended college with my son he was an important motivator for me. I attended the same bible college and my son helped me write my term papers, and God blessed the union of my son and I to become closer on a spiritual level. Once my son and I became closer, to God, we graduated from Bible College together. It has been one of the most rewarding events in my life.

My son received his bachelor's degree in his second year, and I received my associate's degree in biblical studies in my first year at Bible College. Around this time my son and I became volunteer chaplains at Froedtert Medical College, one of the best hospitals in the country.

When my son and I are together, when we are riding in the car together to our destination I have my son read the bible to me, I feel it is important that my son and I stay equipped with the word of God in our heart, and mind daily. Words cannot describe how I feel about my son and I growing closer together spiritually.

I am so proud of what my son has been able to accomplish, especially with all the odds stacked up against him. But I'm even more proud of what we have been able to accomplish together as father and son.

We have volunteered at a soup kitchen together, we helped feed over 1,000 homeless people (it was Marquis idea). He said "Dad we are reading this Bible all the time that is God's word. God's son, Jesus Christ, was a servant. We need to be servants like Jesus in order to be one step closer, to being in the image and likeness of our father. We need to be like the father's son, Jesus, and be a humble servant and help others in need."

I don't think I would have done most of the humanitarian acts that I have if my son wasn't in my life. I thank the Lord my savior, for the great, humanitarian things, I have been able to do together with my son. I consider myself a very lucky man. I believe one of the reasons God put Marquis in my life was to make me a better person.

Before I was a man, running the rat race, I loved my family, but it was all about how much money, I could make. At the end of the day, I was fighting to stay on top and help my son with his autism.

I think autism was a way for God to show me that there is more to life than making money, and wining, the rat race. My son, Marquis and I have become more spirit filled and spirit led, and we are becoming more involved in our local church.

Being involved positively has helped our spiritual life and attitude immensely. My son and I want to be an example, and start our own father and son ministry, and show other fathers and sons what you can accomplish together when your spirit is directed and led by the power of God.

BLACK CHILDREN AND AUTISM
The Difference is Black and White

Why Are our Black Children Being Diagnosed with Autism
Later than White Children?

By Brandi Tape from bet.com

African American children with autism are being diagnosed almost two years later than children of any other ethnic group, holding up their treatment and in turn their quality of life, according to research.

The average White child is diagnosed around six years old, while Black children are not diagnosed until they're almost eight. It may only seem like a small difference in time, but early treatment is the key to reducing the challenges parents stand to face ahead. It's been found that though most Black parents start asking their pediatrician questions around the two years old mark, they're usually brushed aside and told that the child will be fine or that they are just a late bloomer.

Autism is a disorder that causes children to lag behind other children in terms of speech, behavior and the way they develop, as well as dealing with everyday tasks. Common early warning signs are noticing your child seems to have trouble with hearing you or chatting with you. It can be diagnosed at as early as 18 months, but it's easy for it to go undetected because the aggressive, hyper, eccentric behavior and habits related to autism can easily be viewed as misbehavior.

The most well-known type of autism is autistic disorder, which affects the way children communicate and interact in social situations, but there are four other spectrums of this disorder. Children with Asperger's Syndrome share the social issues that the ones with autistic disorder deal with, but they don't have any language issues and score normal to above average on intelligence tests. Rett Syndrome is usually found in girls who start off with average development but begin to lose skills around ages one and four, while children with childhood disintegrative disorder don't lose skills, until even later, usually beginning long after the children are two. Not all cases are cut and dry, though, and a child with symptoms from more than one of the spectrums may have pervasive developmental disorder, which takes symptoms from every group.

When white children were misdiagnosed with autism they were usually told they had ADHD, but Mandell discovered that Black autistic children were told they had things like psychoses, mental retardation or selective mutism. This, along with the fear that Black parents have of reporting their child's behavioral issues due to the fact that their children are removed from the home as a result more often, makes it hard for Black children with autism to get the treatment that they need.

No one knows exactly what causes autism, but it's been linked to irregularities in the brain. (There is also a school of thought that believes the disease is related to vaccinations, but that research has been widely debunked.) Right now there's no cure for the disorder, but the two more classic types of treatments for autism are counseling, to help the child develop the speaking and social skills they're missing, and medication. Some of the prescriptions given are the same as those prescribed to patients with anxiety, depression or obsessive-compulsive disorder. In severe cases an antipsychotic may even be prescribed.

If you think your child may have autism, your first step is to make an appointment with your pediatrician. Your child will be evaluated to see if they've reached the developmental milestones that a child at their age should have.

Here are a few tips for parents with autistic children:

—Learn everything you can about autism. The more you know the easier it will be to manage and understand your child.

—Keep a journal of every supplement, behavior and treatment. It will help when you're tracking the causes and effects during new treatments.

Used with permission from bet.com

ABOUT THE AUTHOR

Marquis Antwan Garner (featured in photo on the right, next to his father) is a 34-year-old autistic young man from Milwaukee, Wisconsin. He is a Special Olympics athlete who participates in basketball, bowling, soccer, and track. Marquis likes to write creative stories in his spare time. He is an actor, and has been in local stage plays, including *Voice of the Fatherless Child*. He also has been cast as an extra in a few local Milwaukee movies.

Marquis knows that at the present moment there is no known cure for his disease, but he stays positive by keeping himself busy. Marquis describes this as a test. He says, "I've always been tested, not just by my disability, but by life. Kids are cruel – If they didn't try to make me feel bad about my disability, it would be something else – like being black or having dark skin."

Marquis was the first African American in his Special Education class. He says, "Kids analyze everything. A kid with mild Down's Syndrome recalled meeting my mother. He asked our Special

Education teacher if I was adopted, LOL." Marquis has very dark skin and having a mother so light-skinned made some people wonder why he is so dark. The same kid told the teacher he didn't like Marquis because he looks like black males who get arrested on the news.

Being the only black person in his Special Education class was a political minefield for Marquis. All of those experiences have humbled him and made him appreciate the little innocent things in life. "I am touched by people who were told that they couldn't do something, but are still able to overcome them!", says Marquis.

He was told he could not attend college, but he accomplished that dream. Marquis says it helps all human beings stand a better chance of success and happiness if they set goals for themselves. "If you can't walk, you can use crutches or wheelchair; if you can't speak, they have machines or Sign Language to help you; if you have poor handwriting like me – my handwriting is illegible so I use a computer to get my point across."

Marquis understands autism is something he has to live with; he has accepted this and he embraces it. Having the disease makes him pay attention to strangers who have challenges in their own lives as well. Marquis said he was watching an ESPN-TV special about a TNT-TV sports commentator named Ernie Johnson. The documentary told of his courageous victory in overcoming cancer and adopting and raising a son with Duchenne muscular dystrophy.

"I would like to meet Ernie's son, Michael," says Marquis. Marquis was told Michael would probably only live about 12 years. He has lived past that age and fought a tremendous battle to stay alive; although I don't know him I would like to meet him and thank him for being a true inspiration of strength and courage.

In closing, Marquis would like to encourage all the people living with autism around the world and to thank everyone who takes the time to read, research understand the disease. He would also like to thank Joe Bednarek, a good friend in college who helped and tutored him when he struggled with his biblical studies; and his friend Adriel Rich who offered him spiritual guidance. He also wants to thank his friends Maurice McClinton, Brice Johnson Brown and best friend for 20 years, James Patterson. Thanks also go out to Uncle Greg Garner, and a special dedication goes to both the Garner and the Jackson families, the Payne family, the Dunlap family, Charles Jones, Kimberly Jones and Great Aunt Norma Jones, respectfully. Marquis Antwan Garner loves you all and appreciates the impact you all have had in his life. God Bless you all.

CPSIA information can be obtained
at www.ICGtesting.com
Printed in the USA
LVHW07s0840020918
588584LV00007B/7/P